HAL•LEONARD INSTRUMENTAL PLAY-ALONG

ALTO SAX

Chart Hits

CONTENTS

2 All About That Bass MEGHAN TRAINOR
4 All of Me JOHN LEGEND
6 Happy PHARRELL WILLIAMS
8 Radioactive IMAGINE DRAGONS
10 Roar KATY PERRY
12 Say Something A GREAT BIG WORLD
16 Shake It Off TAYLOR SWIFT
18 A Sky Full of Stars COLDPLAY
13 Someone Like You ADELE
24 Stay with Me SAM SMITH
20 Thinking Out Loud ED SHEERAN
22 Uptown Funk MARK RONSON FEATURING BRUNO MARS

To access audio visit:
www.halleonard.com/mylibrary

Enter Code
8380-9308-2584-5934

Audio Arrangements by Peter Deneff

ISBN 978-1-4950-2302-6

T0056125

HAL•LEONARD® CORPORATION
7777 W. BLUEMOUND RD. P.O. BOX 13819 MILWAUKEE, WI 53213

ALL ABOUT THAT BASS

ALTO SAX

Words and Music by KEVIN KADISH
and MEGHAN TRAINOR

3
3
3
To Coda
D.S. al Coda
CODA

ALL OF ME

ALTO SAX

Words and Music by JOHN STEPHENS
and TOBY GAD

To Coda
D.S. al Coda
CODA
mp
mf
p

HAPPY

from DESPICABLE ME 2

ALTO SAX

Words and Music by
PHARRELL WILLIAMS

RADIOACTIVE

ALTO SAX

Words and Music by DANIEL REYNOLDS,
BENJAMIN McKEE, DANIEL SERMON,
ALEXANDER GRANT and JOSH MOSSER

mp
1.
2.
cresc.
f

ROAR

ALTO SAX

Words and Music by KATY PERRY,
LUKASZ GOTTWALD, MAX MARTIN,
BONNIE McKEE and HENRY WALTER

To Coda
D.S. al Coda
CODA
2
mf
f

SAY SOMETHING

ALTO SAX

Words and Music by IAN AXEL,
CHAD VACCARINO and MIKE CAMPBELL

SOMEONE LIKE YOU

ALTO SAX

Words and Music by ADELE ADKINS
and DAN WILSON

f
To Coda
D.S. al Coda

CODA
mf
rit.
mf–f
a tempo
1.
2.
mf
p
4

SHAKE IT OFF

ALTO SAX

Words and Music by TAYLOR SWIFT,
MAX MARTIN and SHELLBACK

2.
D.S. al Coda
CODA
8
1.
2.
1.
2.
1.
2.

A SKY FULL OF STARS

ALTO SAX

Words and Music by GUY BERRYMAN,
JON BUCKLAND, WILL CHAMPION,
CHRIS MARTIN and TIM BERGLING

Moderate Dance groove

ff
1., 2.
3.
D.S. al Coda
CODA
ff
Play 4 times
f
4
mf
2
mp

THINKING OUT LOUD

ALTO SAX

Words and Music by ED SHEERAN
and AMY WADGE

f
To Coda
D.S. al Coda
CODA

UPTOWN FUNK

ALTO SAX

Words and Music by MARK RONSON,
BRUNO MARS, PHILIP LAWRENCE,
JEFF BHASKER, DEVON GALLASPY
and NICHOLAUS WILLIAMS

mf
f
f
To Coda
D.S. al Coda
(with repeats)
CODA
1.–3.
4.

STAY WITH ME

ALTO SAX

Words and Music by SAM SMITH,
JAMES NAPIER and WILLIAM EDWARD PHILLIPS